About the Author

Hello! I'm sixteen years old living in the north of England. Poetry has always given me a safe space to process my thoughts and emotions, being there during highs and lows. I wrote this book during late December evenings when the moon's soft light would peek out between my blinds, which is why I wrote so many poems about her! I hope you appreciate her beauty as much as I do, and I hope her presence brings you peace during tough times.

The Moon and Other Poems

Shree Bhattacharjee

The Moon and Other Poems

Olympia Publishers
London

www.olympiapublishers.com
OLYMPIA PAPERBACK EDITION

A CIP catalogue record for this title is
available from the British Library.

ISBN: 978-1-80074-344-1

This is a work of fiction.
Names, characters, places and incidents originate from the writer's
imagination. Any resemblance to actual persons, living or dead, is
purely coincidental.

First Published in 2021

Olympia Publishers
Tallis House
2 Tallis Street
London
EC4Y 0AB
Printed in Great Britain

Dedication

This book is dedicated to my wonderful parents, Sanchita and Chanchal, for their silver anniversary.

Acknowledgements

Thank you to my family for helping me to find my love in poetry and giving me the courage to write this book. Thank you for the immense love you gave me, and the sacrifices you dealt with so I could pursue my wishes. Thank you to the amazing team of Olympia publishers, who has made my dreams come true. And lastly, thank you to the reader for buying my work. Thank you for telling me there are more people in this world with a similar brain to mine.

EBONY

You always hated your dark hair, feared you never
contained her flair, always admired her golden mane as
you called yours mundane.
But you never saw beneath the black, and failed to realise
that
Her hair may erupt with the sun's rays,
But yours twinkle with the moon's gaze.
Her hair may capture the bloom of light, whereas yours
shines in the depths of the night. She may have the
colours of ember and gold, but you have masses of
stories untold.
Of your raven mane and your midnight tresses which
gleam with timeless beauty,
And swirl with endless profundity
Of the grandeur carried in one single strand.

AFTER IT RAINS

why do they call it melancholy?
when petrichor wafts through open windows
and moss twinkles with dew drops

do they not see beauty in glinting branches?
like stars in a constellation

why do they not sympathise
with the leaves while they shake tears off
as the sky weeps

do they not notice
the satisfied rumbles of thunder before he vanishes for
our happiness

but surely they don't realise that nature only blossoms
after it rains.

HER

Look up the word
— Woman —
what they say is fake.
You cannot define woman.
Woman is so complex, we fail to comprehend.
Her sheer beauty, intelligence, extravagance masculinity.
An indescribable, indestructible force
— we take so long to discover.
Because she cannot be put into a single category, Woman
is everything.

COLD MISTY MORNINGS

The night caves in
and I go
to the place where my memories glisten like
raindrops on a cold February morning
and the injured leaves
crackling as I trample across the frosted mud
like on a cold February morning
headphones in
wispy hair strewn into a loose plait
hands quivering
like on that cold February morning
when I first laid my eyes on

You

SELENE

I see her in my dreams:
A slender figure dressed in white;
Her shoulders droop as she silently weeps,
On her balcony in the stealth of night.

Slowly she begins to notice me,
And curiously beckons me; forth
My eyes adjust to her beauty;
She embraces me in all her warmth.

We stand together amidst the dark;
Her bony fingers laced around my hair.
Cheeks pressed against mine, leaves a mark;
Her breath misty in frozen air.

Waters glint with the moon's gaze;
Clouds sweep the midnight skies.
A single tear descends from her slate eyes ablaze;
With all the world's raging blizzards and ice.

We watch as the emerging sun mends our broken hearts;
Rays unveil the early wisps of dawn.
The moon beings to hide behind her counterpart;
Unmasking her empathy as we quietly mourn.

We sigh sweetly, as the golden rays cascade…
Onto the willowed trees silvery and pale;
But she gently pushes against my weight;
Stepping back all fragile and frail.

A small sad look washes across her face,
As I helplessly whisper 'don't leave';
She shimmers and vanishes without a trace,
Granting time for me to grieve.

THE CONVENTIONAL ROOFTOP OF PARIS

I like to sit up here on hot summer nights…
In a reverie of nostalgia
Of a past life or a distant memory,
Dazed by the plethora of glimmers,
The Eiffel winks at me,
And his fellow rustic street lamps.

I watch the clouds unfold their mood swings —
On my poor victimised soul,
As 2 or 3 cold droplets slide down my arm,
Frosting my comfort
Sometimes I cry with them,
My neighbour's Merlot in hand, Swigging away with
disrespect,
I should have brought a table and chairs, and a candle I
guess.

These Parisians romanticise too much
Smoking on adorned balconies
Depicting the anguish of Chopin
On baby grands at the crack of dawn.
They love extravagantly,
And hurt unbearably,
But that's what sets them apart from the rest of the world.

Because when everyone expects prosperity —
They always expect a tragedy.

YOU AGAIN

The moon studies you, As I do too;
You're basking in the radiance — Of her lim lit stare;
We both cannot look away; You're the epitome of
ethereal…
Prancing through the streets at 1 am;
Your dress billowing around you in the slight breeze;
Chipped nail varnish gleaming under street lamps;
A thrifted jacket engulfing your willowy shoulders, I
watch but I cannot help…
but think —
What I had done in a past life,
To deserve you?

YOKO

They named you the child of the sun,

Crafted by his rays

which burst out of your sickly-sweet heart,

burning holes of anger.

scorching your kindness
into fury and madness,

you made a mistake even putting yourself out

There,

you didn't realise it at the time,

your poor brain failed to console your
breath taking soul — that

each time you would get attracted to his zeal,

you would seethe into nothing.

UNVEILING

I don't think you realise,
the immense wisdom you hold.
in those endless holes that
swirl into the deepest parts of your soul,
exposing the raw nature of your beauty,

exposing the real you.

galaxies of pain, sadness, love… As you look into mine.
and look away. don't look away.

I would like to see the real you.

ASTRAEA

They always singled her out, and praised her charm, She
stood out in vast crowds Dwelling soft and calm,
She gleamed amongst companions, dress rippling in the
wind.
She caught the jealousy of swans, and the admiration of
our kin.
She radiated within us,
But would often disappear too.
For it was always a solace to see one whom
We so anguished to lose.
I'd often step into my garden, and look up at the
crepuscular sky
Overwhelmed with tranquillity, as she shone for millions
of miles.
I'd blurt all my worries,
And lament into the night. She looked at me wisdom,
And assured me it would be all right.
Her wistful pure aura,
Brought me nothing but bliss,
As she left me one last time,
Savouring what I could reminisce.

GAIA

Thick brown locks brush against sweet smelling soil,
Barefoot in deep thick mud.
Fingers trailing delicately over whispers of leaves, Which
drip with sap as abundant as blood.
She mutters her daily continuity with
winds tracing her every stride,
They fly high through the seas and the heavens,
Yet careful not to anger the tides.
Her amber eyes gaze over her garden
Of evergreen fields forests and streams
Which web their way into her skin, And her heart and into
her dreams.
A caramel complexion complete with chestnut hair,
Her solid beauty contains flecks of gold.
Yet despite her mellow secure stature,
There lies an endless horizon of steel and cold.
For we underestimate the power,
The sheer devastation that is contained,
With a careless flick of a finger,
Comes disastrous cyclones and unrelenting rains.
The pounding of her heart
Sends seizures past surfaces,
The quick turn of a head
Torments gusts and crevices.
She weeps in frustration, tears splashing from her

distressed eyes,
As floods sweep the roads,
And monsoons pour from the skies. We provoke her, do
we not?
And prod at her very veins
Where her beauty is annihilated,
who else but us is to blame?

FOR YOUR MELANCHOLY POETRY SESSIONS

The candle
In its temporary glory
Flourishes with a delicate hue.
The hue of late night coffee extravagances;
And cigarette smoke billowing from your window in the
stealth of an autumn night.
Fingers stained with royal blue ink smeared over the
cracked pages
Of the small leather notebook which you hold so dear,
Which houses your wondrous inclinations.
Notions you are crazy to believe that can change the
world; Yet
The ones who truly think they can change the world are
the ones who do?
Rachmaninoff flows into 1am
2 am;
As you dream about your future lover,
Who will dance endless waltzes around mahogany piano
notes floating in air.
Your auburn hair smoothed back into a plait
With the ribbon you cherish,
The wine-coloured fabric
Cut off from a Christmas present,
Years ago.

The patter of nightly rain occurs
As you step out to your rusted balcony,
And look up into the gloom of clouds,
And the moon
Whose gaze always haunts you.
Because you remember a time when you looked up to her
Without a single care.

These splashes comfort you, Somehow.
They remind you of being washed,
Being purified
Of your sins which you cannot even remember doing.
Yet you pretend you are so dark, when really the sins you
commit
Are during your melancholy poetry sessions.

HAZY

the mornings pass me by
fuelled with bleary eyes and tousled hair,
I scratch into my journal,
it's really only the soft yellow pages that seem to care.

mist lingers from yesternight's disorder — of rattling
windows, wailing winds,
trees cry for help from never ending tumult,
they etch my dark circles deeper in skin.

an opaque breeze seems to fill my lungs
of a frangible winter's day,
crisp leaves and beckoning benches,
a sky filmy and grey.

SUMMER ROMANTICISED

I dream of a summer in paradise — of garden parties,
the sound of tea cups rattling,
Linen dresses ebbing in slight gusts.
The graceful turn of pages
Of Elio and Oliver…
Pining for 1983.
As we glide through rivers,
Totes swaying off branches,
And sunglasses buried in a myriad of button downs,
Could you just imagine?
Your honey voice chirping sweet sounding strings of
letters
On our front porch at dusk,
Lazily swatting at flies.
Sighing,
Smiling,
tranquillised into late afternoon naps.

FATA MORGANA

Sometimes I open my eyes to see a man sitting beside me.
Normally he lives at the bottom of my mind
Edging, prodding into my skin.
Sometimes we joke about my helpless future, scribbling
away on straps of paper.
Prancing, linking hands to our favourite tunes, sobbing as
they strap me in.
His guidance is a blessing;
My only true comfort in a plethora of havoc
Inciting my mania,
Shredding newly healed scars. He is

my pain, my love.

He draws for me,
Leaving small sticky notes around the place.
Mother looks terrified when I introduce him?
She can't see his shimmering beauty.
My pristine angel,
The beginnings of my conflict.
He's very unreliable though,
Because the times when I am at my very worst,
He is never there.

LIBERATED

I am
Ensnared by the wires of my tension,
Pushing them to the back of the room.
Bubbling and frothing on the brink of overflow,
Whilst I grip the noose,
That delicately grazes this cauldron,
Of disturbance and quiet —
One step away from eruption.

Please facilitate my flight,
Lift this barrier
Which prevents me from seeing them.
Rescue me from this enclosing cell,
Liberate me.

THE GHOST

In my attic lives a woman Of iridescent and silver
Who traces the hallways at night,
And resides back to her brooding place at day.
I have tried to befriend her…
Immersed
by an enchantress who refuses to even look at me,
No matter the time.
In the evenings I retire to my piano,
I cannot play very well so I shut the door.
But today I decide to leave it open, Tinkering with a few
bad compositions.
Moments later she drifts in
Enraptured by my notes,
A shy smile spreads across her face,
Ushering me to carry on.
In a few minutes she offers to duet,
Perched shimmering beside me,
As we play a familiar piece.
And smile a familiar smile,
Her piano sings like never before,
As we play a polonaise,
Our hands race across the rusted edges
Long past twilight.
Our late night conversations occur daily,
As we compare childhoods and memories. She tells me

about my grandparents —

And sings me to eternal sleep.

CONFINEMENT

dance with me,
let us free away from its snaring grip,
as it slowly swathes us Until we suffocate.
Trapped inside closing walls,
mirrors reflecting our debilitated shapes,
as we gauchely climb from our wretched beds,
and link hands—
oh wait!
we aren't supposed to link hands, are we?
let us whirl,
eyes closed,
feet bare,
a chaotic descent into
madness.

WINTER NIGHTS

Walking through dim lit streets snake through a city, I call
my nest
Souls lurking past fogged windows.
Their gauzy figures carved into frosted air,
Lampposts glare with grave expressions Staring down as
snowflakes glitter my nose,
Spiralling into my curls
Ice cold and exposed.
I pull on my coat,
Frictionless gloves on dampened fleece,
Gasping,
Choking on bitter air particles
As I look up at industrialised giants, icicles on pipes,
And frost on glazings.
The nights seem to engulf us all, Stars staying away from
our affairs, As their innocence twinkles aons away,
Observing the tranquil after Christmas dinner,
The rigidity in our daily walks,
And the tautness that we bring into the new year.

7 DEVILS

Escape with me —
Into a universe of mythical lands.
Let us dive into —
A bottomless pit of sorcery.
You unleash your hidden immaturity, 'As they say';
And waltz through abandoned castles in ripped ballgowns.
After smothering Charming;
Sharpen our guilted knives.
While we sacrifice in nebulous woods
Descending into a chaos of occultism, And evil incarnate
Don't forget.
I mean I don't want to repeat the obvious;
The devils are masked as angels.

HOW I PICTURE A LAKESIDE AFTERNOON

The blades beckon me,
Swaying to the beat of midsummer.

On a hot afternoon, dragonflies curiously approach.

My cats nuzzle in the shade,
I look down at my reflection.

Watch the blurred lines merge into a sunburnt face,
Earrings gleaming and freckles checking in.

The sun waves at me,
Rays stroking my picnic basket.
Blinding me in my white dress, He decides to descend.
The starlings agreeing and chirp goodbye, as I bask in the
flickering warmth
Of rocking chairs and front porches,
And lazy grins.

NOSTALGIA

deep inside my heart lives a hole — of lost kisses and
laughter.
far-flung songs, giggles,
forgotten festivities.
in good times the hole heals,
only to be punctured.
by a familiar smell,
a cherished taste,
and the resurfacing of memories of you.

GUMUSSERVI

Imagine a painting that floats in visions, listlessly, you
can't grasp the meaning. You're drawn to it, however,
Enraptured by the traces of ethereality crossing your
mind every few days,
You see a mirror of faint glows,
Surrounded by perpetual shadows, you're unable to see
the source.
The hope.
You see it's like a jigsaw.
It's like seeing your soulmate at airports, basking in the
time you have
to appreciate snippets of artistry, glimpses of intense
ambedo.

CONTRAST

A complete blur
Scattered notes failing my poor eyes,
Hands swift as they dash into my face, childish frolics
With deep meaning,
blending and merging,
Like when I mix droplets of watery paint, watching them
make their mark on paper,
As the tone rips isolated air into two, when we look at life
the way we see them,
Many of the world's problems would terminate.

GRAVEYARD

Walking over your bodies fills me with shame, Tears
creeping out onto pallid cheeks.
As I brush moss follicles and dust away to read the words
endeared and 1917.

I often sit quietly as lingering mist leaves to expose a
limitless canvas of gloom, picking at the weeds that
interweave
Down to your soul where melancholy blooms!

I wonder if you are at peace,
A tormented mind fleeing at unrest.
I hope you smile with that carefree ease that I saw of you
in your ivory dress, soaking up coveted sunlight.
And you now lie here in shadows,
We both long for the crispness of twilight.

I TOLD THE STARS ABOUT YOU

i told the stars about you.
you, in your uttermost opulence,
a being too transcendental to grace this land, a celestial
presence
to remind me everyday, make me writhe in graciousness.
how you chose *me*
me?
An innocent passerby,
preyed upon by a waif like creature who tossed away my
besotted eyes?
trapped me in an ice palace of manipulation in your
remorseless, cerulean ones.
so yes, yes, I told the stars about you,
they're the only other beings to know the real you!

MOON GAZING

I think of her a lot.
I write about her a lot.
I wonder of her a lot.

Wrapped in a cocoon of bedsheets
Of chamomile tea and sleep drenched eyes,
The clouds wafting away for us all to see.

I adore her unpredictability, her mischief. Masked behind
her many divine forms,
And every night I sigh in disbelief.

Scars drilled into her carefully sculpted face, and a veil of
gauzy layers of lace.

Admiring her grace from far away,
Forever pondering upon the stories she could say.

OLD PHOTO

I would do anything for old school love. For diners and
Demeanour.
Late night telephone calls, giggling beside the record
player.
Dances in my kitten heels,
Coming home to a drunk mess,
demands for missed affection,
Wondering how long it's taking them to come back while I
sit still and look pretty.

I would do anything for old school love?

VENUS

i beg of you,
guide me through.

the unfamiliarity that can be seen,
dwellings no one has ever been.

in the deepest cages of my heart,
if you could only rip me apart.

and repress me whole,
where I could nestle and console.

relieved I could never be broken,
and dive into waters foreign
to my soul.

THUNDERSTORM

You're the raging ocean to my weak flickers.
I may cry before you,
But you always leave a mark,
As you grouse and sing your blues,
And everyone drapes onto your lingering letters,
Scarcely acknowledging mine.
They regard me with fear,
Look at you with sympathy curling in their brains, and
cast me aside.
I don't mean to hurt them,
And you apologise time and time again.
While I sit suppressed Motionless,
Caught in spirals of your operation,
And I sulk.
My tension builds up,
While you approach me,
Sighing.

I've done it again

I'm tired of your lectures,
helpless
Disappearing from so many places, I could count for
Just for your comfort.

DESPERATE YOUTH

you may agonise with us,
but strip us of our freedom,
and trap us.
from even ephemeral moments of happiness,
we pace in our rooms
immobile, stiff, braced
to ponder over our existence, you've lived these years
with liberty.
don't tell us it's our fault we're wasting ours.

THE WATERFALL FAIRY (IN THE EYES OF THE NARRATOR)

I look up to see her,
A face scrunched in fascination.
She leans gently, her hair,
An eternal droop of ultramarine blending into a rock
pool of life,
And fat droplets glistening off her pulsing temples.
Artistic wrists tracing pebbles,
A sticky satin dress clinging to her glass skin, I fear she
will fall,
And shatter into a spoon drift.
She pushes her shoulders into thick moss
Grounded in steam.
A perfect picture of serenity
With a tinkle
Sprays a prism in my direction, Dancing eyes edging my
Retaliation,
I sing with the dryads.
Her cheeks placid, she hums along.
Showers drenching our hair and mirth dousing our
Worries, the winds sway to our beat
Foam crackling in the corners.
Whispering to the clouds to run away.

THE WATERFALL FAIRY (DO WE REALLY KNOW HER?)

She would often look down at her pool
To hear nymphs, giggle and dryads squeal.
She wished for no responsibilities
And sense the childish bliss that they could feel.
the winds would often ground her,
gusts pressing her back against rock.
every time she would lean forward,
frosted puffs would give her a shock.
an eternal droop of ultramarine
blended into a cove of youth
whose sublimity was also her curse
that no other fairy could soothe.
for she was bound there for the rest of her life,
humming to obliviate the time that passed by.
if she fell she would shatter into spoon drift,
and cast eternal showers and prisms up in the sky

RENDEZVOUS

Hello,
Hello?
I don't think we've met before?
Whenever I appear, you're never around.
Whenever I emerge, you always leave,
Separated by constellations
and clouds.
My name is Aelia.
I am Celeste.
I suppose we are soulmates.

FLEETED MOMENTS

She dreamed of light pressing onto her back, Warm flares
lapping up her dark hair
nursed by a blaze of beams.
He dreamed of cold wintery glows,
Pearl brilliance contrasted into black,
And glittering auras bathing his tanned skin.
It would be long before they could meet again.

ALLEGORY OF THE APOCALYPSE

Eyes blazing and tears held back, I look in awe —
At your divinely presence storming the skies, wings
beating to the rhythm of cries
As they shrink back.
Hands pressed against strained eyes
As we escape the demons beneath us, you lift us up into
the clouds.
As I soar past legends, Fables fabricated into time.
I reach out to stroke their hair, Struck by their aura.
As you let go
A barrier of brick wall behind those eyes, as you watch
me dive into
The hell that awaits me,
The demons that continue to haunt me
Back into soil.

THE ACCOLADE

I have never seen such steel behind a figure, Outlined in
silver and opaline snow.
Her auburn hair floating underneath a crown, Forged in
dungeons in blazes of inferno.
Her eyes command my knees to drop, Bathed by her
seraphic rays.
Skin glowing with such luminance, My poor mortal eyes
have to look away.
Her sword presses against shaking shoulders, I pray to
god that I may not break.
A being so mystic, from the Otherworld… One glance at
her face would be a mistake.
My clumsy rise does not prepare me for what I see and
behold,
The warnings of her beauty have not cast over,
Nor have the stories and wisdom that were told.
My lady regards me
With curiosity of a kind.
A hint of a smile vanishes,
And so does my state of mind.

EVENING READS

Behind the wheels of her pupils Lived a mischievous little
girl.
Havoc dancing at the tips of her fingertips,
Who would often peek behind her evening glasses,
And cause internal mayhem,
And occasionally
She would smile.

FEATURES

If they even knew,
That our faces hold legacies of ancestry
Those that stood before yours, Their unique features
That you so chose to point at, And satirise.
While we canopy our 'imperfections',
And lighten our skin
So that we can be somewhere near as 'beautiful',
As you.

DRIED FLOWERS

Because I miss notebook annotations, and late-night verse
readings,
And picking them from the forbidden glade, the scent of
satisfaction
As we press them to our noses. Fingers lingering on their
light and life
Their last remaining beauty
Snaps.

FORBIDDEN FRUIT

Tiptoeing
Around rasping hinges, and discordant
Floorboards, She hushes us.
If the patriarchy ever finds out…
And we stroke fine leather
Imprints of years of bygone times, fingers squashing
creasing mouths,
We read the first few dusted pages, and bewail
Of having been deprived for so long
Of the sweet sensation of cultivation,
Seeping through noses sniffing
Torn pages,
Sap dripping down columns and
Regret.

If only we would've been born differently.

STUDIO APARTMENT

To buy: Sage vase, Vintage quilt, Window chalk,
Flower pressed frames, coffee table, books, pillows,
silk throws.
Plushies for lonely nights, glow in the dark stars,
Paints and old music for sudden obsessions — Anything
to distract me from you.
But we're so alike,
It's never going to work.

BLANK CANVAS

This is going to be direct.
I measure it up for half an hour;
I focus on it… I try to, at least.
Imagining the glory;
Trying to forget the next few hours;
Paints oozing in my periphery; Judging my lack of
organisation;
As I slash them across the surface
Is it anger? destruction? elation? allurement?
I can't stand abstract paintings.

MY FOREHEAD PRESSED AGAINST GLASS

you slide down my window,
etching tunnels into condensation, you're
like veins across my arm
swivelling and merging.
i plead for you to win; you entwine with another;
circling the other with caution; i'm at my wits end
i'm rooting for you.
you're hesitant, you don't think this is the path,
for you.
this wasn't supposed to be the end,
you stop.
my disappointment is fleeting,
as I breathe hearts out in front of you.
staring at your fellow contestants… shaking
in feverishness.
maybe they will accept their swift ending?
who knows.

COTTAGE

in the hills of my daydreams, we frolic in the fields
of sweet-smelling lavender, and bonnets that yield.

to the winds that dance around us,
hushing our cries by the stream,
vintage dresses tipped with minerals
failing to catch fish that weave,
swift past our darkened hands.
from lurking beside the ponds,
complete with contrasting efflorescences,
the homes of nymphs and beyond.
the crevices of lumbering pillars
lives the wise old maid,
from the adventures of the faraway tree
of Silky and Moon Face.

BOOKSTORES

I sit on the steps
Glancing up at you from time to time.
You in your coffee duster and espresso jumper, glasses
perched on a perfect bridge.
As you flick through them
Like the flapping of feathers in the sunset,
Occasionally casting hints of grins, I sip my tea.

Sorting through wooden shelves,
And their years of stories hidden behind ripped suede
casings.
That old book smell wafting past, every time I unlock a
veiled novel.
Side glances do not even catch your interest,
Concealed in a trance of fantasy. It's really a tragic drama,
That I can never pluck up the resilience as you stroll out
of here like you always do.
I sip my tea.

EXOTIC

It's funny how
You deem my appearance as unusual.
When my people are more populated than yours, my
culture
with a bigger mark than yours. You consider me
with sympathy,
As you praise yours,
Belittle mine,
Small remarks on how to improve mine,
And your ignorant self carries on, while my exotic self
hides away.

FAIRY TEA PARTY

I was walking through the woods, when I heard twitters
and clinks of acorn teacups,
And blackberry drinks.
I peeped through the bushes, rubbing my eyes to see—
An array of fae.
In a midsummer evening's dream,
Sprinkles of glitter hung in the air, wings perched on
sheaths of grass
Fluttering through teapots and silver jugs.
A feast of many midsummers past,
They wished the children a goodnight's sleep, And the
adults an extra dose of luck.
As they dined on cherry strudels and cheesecake pops,
And raspberry water in mushroom mugs,
Soon the fireflies lit up,
And the sun decided to part,
Linen tables of fruit shone—
The midsummer dance was about to start.
The fae began to link hands,
Mesmerised, I viewed a phenomenon,
But I closed my eyes to take all in—
And when I opened them there were none.

PERSEPHONE

I've seen you strolling in my garden, tawny ringlets
entwine your face, and I can't help but envy your striking
melanin glistening on this warm spring dawn.

An image of mildness and you Incandesce in your rose
dress, While petals flap around you.

Like your own gale,
Like the geese that glide over blaze meadows, and plop at
your feet,
Squawking for attention and weave their necks into the
nook of your elbow,
And you sit down in grace On a stone bench,
To escape their wrath, their squabbles for glory,
you escape —
Amongst vines and roses,

And sit for a while.

I HELD A STAR IN MY HAND

I held a star in my hand,
He quivered and took shelter in my palm.
Jagged breaths and puffs of dust,
Though it took a while to ease him and calm.

He lay there with a forlorn expression, Upturned smile
had begun to droop.
He focused above with such pain in his face,
As we regarded millions of clusters and groups.

He told me he couldn't recognise the asterisms, Orion had
never even bothered to raise his bow, Andromeda was
nowhere to be seen,
Sirius only looked on with the faintest glow.

I assured him this was only mourning,
His lustrous tears dribbling down blanched cheeks.
His fall was so dramatic, a swivelling shot of light which
faded until —
He was nowhere, to be seen.

POST ITS

It's always been grocery lists. To do lists.
Self-care lists. Scribble the last one out.
I often think of how much she has endured. Yet I look at
her with so much disdain.
My brain exploiting my mind. Driving her to the back of
the cavity.
Where she lies in chains.
And now my brain has all the power
To turn me against my own skin.

IS IT HEALING?

I know you doubt yourself.
It's an everyday occurrence when you see your wounds,
ingrained on your scratched face.
They never close up, And nor do you unfurl.
Your bud wrapped so tightly, it cocoons you from even
taking baby steps.
And you shield us away.

But we will be there,
We will water you and feed you sunlight.
When a time comes for you to emerge, and bloom
a little later.

OUTER SPACE

Could you imagine
A void
So silent?
The breaths devour you.
You don't even focus on your breathing. Instead, it's the
planets, which scrutinise
this dot of existence.
You forget to breathe
Spiralling fogs,
Pits,
Craters
Nebulae.
In this trichiliocosm,
You dare not even think about
What could be out there.

VIDE

i look at her staring back at me
i'm helpless, distraught,
vacant sockets,
hollowed cheeks,
they protrude out,
pointing haphazardly in all directions.
ashen skin sealing my desolate conscience,
the glass seems to agree,
unfolding one pocket after another,
shining light onto

that thing —
that dreaded thing that consumes my sanity,
clicking away like a typewriter.
penciling fluctuations
failing to ever make me pacified.
my frustration is solely dependent on that
machine,
who reads me everyday
critiquing 50
40
30
20
10
0

Before you carry on reading, you may notice a difference in the maturity of my writing. I wrote these next six poems at different stages while growing up. Some were written when I was nine, some written when I was thirteen. I decided to place these poems in for you and I both to experience a feeling of immaturity to take a break from the serious matters I have written about earlier.

AM I GOOD ENOUGH?

Am I good enough, to be in that social class?
Where someone's self-respect and dignity is as fragile as
glass, Where people go with the new trend,
Looking so unnatural so that they can blend.

Am I good enough, to wear that much? Where cheap
clothing cannot be touched, where it's so in to wear Gucci
and Chanel, with tops so tight that it feels like hell.

Am I good enough, to cake foundation on my face? And
layer on all that primer just to know my place? And tweeze
and tweeze my brows until they are no more, putting on
so much concealer that it feels like a chore.

Am I good enough, to drink all that beer?
When I don't want to but I'm pressured by peers,
where I come home drunk at night,
Giving my parents an awful fright.

Am I good enough, to feel amazing all the time? If I burst
out my feelings, I would do a crime, I'm alone and
depressed, but you don't know, because I'm taking
medications that I don't show.

Am I good enough, to be taking all these pills? Taking all

these substances that can kill,
I have an addiction, you see, so it's hard to stop,
Taking so much that my blood pressure drops.

Am I good enough, to get so many likes,
If I don't, my so-called friends will strike,
And rip my confidence apart until I'm sobbing with pain,
And abuse my social media, throwing it down the drain.

Am I good enough, to be all skin and bone?
To be starving with hunger until I moan?
To lose so much weight and yet seem fine,
When really if I carry on, I could die.

THE GIRL WHO DREW

I once knew a girl
Who etched into her body
Beautiful, intricate drawings on skin,
Carved neatly, so precisely, with utmost care.
So people's worries wouldn't begin,

She sketched and embedded,
She drew day and night,
But she didn't want anyone to know.
So she drew out of sight,

Soon enough I noticed her drawings,
And approached her out of the blue.
She looked at me with pain in her eyes,
But I whispered, 'I draw too.'

SUMMER DAYS

The meadows broadened out to the horizon, swaying in
the breeze, We'd giggle and scramble through them,
finding shade in the trees. Immature and carefree, hair
whispering in the wind,
Thinking of our grandmothers' morals we'd snort and
grin.

We flourished and accelerated through school, a few
beatings you'd receive but I played it cool. Jobs landed; we
both toiled solid hours well,
And I would wait for those summer dusks, for those tales
you'd tell.

Sometimes we would go fishing, ensnaring trout in the
streams, we rode our stallions and your face beamed
With a smile that could illuminate the world like a torch,
It appeared when we'd sip lemon juice on hot days,
relaxing on your front porch.

But winter cropped up and the sun seldom turned out,
To say farewell when you made your choice with no
doubt.
You grasped your father's army coat and packed all your
belongings, And never gave me a chance to say how much
I would yearn for you.

You opened a door to a vision of conflict, decease and
lies, Which affected me the most, yet I smothered those
sighs, Constant storms eradicated the daisies in the
meadows,
And my heart shattered into a million fragments like
windows.

Our friendship fell adrift when I could write no more
letters through pain, But all I could think of were
memories of summer days.

PAINTING

The golden sky stretches out to the horizon, hints of pink
clouds hiding behind gilded rays, The last auburn leaves
fall off the bare branches of gnarled trees,
Endless flocks of birds fly by, forming a continuous array
of patterns at daybreak,
Morning mist clings to the air, twinkling at moonlight.

Delicate snowflakes land on the tips of noses and
tongues, As children squeal while skating on frost-bound
ponds,
The pleasant face of the merry snowman beams at fellow
folk, Until the usual robin comes and takes a nip out of
his carrot.

Evening hours are spent reading classics by the glowing
fire, And the scent of homemade cakes waft through
every household,
Steaming cocoa is drunk while families sit in their snug
woollen jumpers and fleecy socks,
And the sky clears to a midnight blue, only with the subtle
gleams of those astronomical captivations.

EUROPEAN NIGHTS

Do you remember those nights of dimly lit cobblestone
paths,
Winding into the heart of the small towns you so love to
explore of sleek black umbrellas waving about in the
February rain,
Matching with your leather jackets purchased from a
thrift store in the suburbs.
Do you remember the nights of
Cherry lipstick stained on blood red wine,
Casting aside champagne As you sit beside the Seine,
And contemplate running away from your dull
neighbourhood,
and joining French Vogue.
And do you remember silk white dresses billowing in the
late summer breeze,
As you try to learn as many idioms as possible,
To pretend that you're the quintessential native, and nights
Of laughter sounding from the restaurants above the
beach you lie on,
Listening to the ripples of crystal-clear water,
As the tide not only washes your sandals but also your
thoughts away.
Do you remember staggering barefoot On village roads,
After your heels gave way and your stomach inflated from
having 2 pizzas and 3 helpings of the local pasta,

You will never have better pasta ever again.
And nights
exchanging small conversations,
With the old ladies in the towns of primaeval chapels,
As they exclaim how pretty you are but tell you to eat
more.
When you used up all your polaroids Trying to capture the
perfect moment
Of looking nice while trying to eat 3 churros at once, And
those ethereal medieval castles
Surrounded by weaves of grapevines, Weaving in
And out
Of anecdotes and reflections.

BALCONY AT NIGHT

3 in the morning
With teardrops sliding down your cheeks,
Blending in with the rain, A cigarette
Lightly balanced on your fingers, As you watch your
feeble rings
Wash out into the darkness,
You should have never asked for a joint from him.
He is the cause of all your problems, As well as all your
happiness.
You find comfort in nights like these when the sky opens
up all her
troubles to you,
As you lean on the metal railings, and confide in each
other.
He broke me — what you imagine is a scream,
Yet what only comes out is a helpless whisper,
You know you love too much.
You're going to miss these autumn nights
When darkness sits in earlier for you to find solace in,
When you're not pretending to drink out of his
fluorescent bottle.
Music you never liked, People you never knew
On those lazy summer evenings sat by a waterfront which
made you feel like you were in a dream.
These people moved around like ghosts, Their voices

Crying out for more beer.
The moon checks on you for a while
To make sure you're not really dragging one foot after
another off the railing,
As you sometimes wish you'd have the courage to do so.
You throw the cigarette away,
And watch as it descends into a peril of dustbins and
racoons, pulling the sleeves of your jumper,
And head back inside.

Printed in Great Britain
by Amazon